W9-APE-998

George Whitefield

Clergyman and Scholar

Colonial Leaders

Lord Baltimore
English Politician and Colonist

Benjamin Banneker
American Mathematician and Astronomer

Sir William Berkeley
Governor of Virginia

William Bradford
Governor of Plymouth Colony

Jonathan Edwards
Colonial Religious Leader

Benjamin Franklin
American Statesman, Scientist, and Writer

Anne Hutchinson
Religious Leader

Cotton Mather
Author, Clergyman, and Scholar

Increase Mather
Clergyman and Scholar

James Oglethorpe
Humanitarian and Soldier

William Penn
Founder of Democracy

Sir Walter Raleigh
English Explorer and Author

Caesar Rodney
American Patriot

John Smith
English Explorer and Colonist

Miles Standish
Plymouth Colony Leader

Peter Stuyvesant
Dutch Military Leader

George Whitefield
Clergyman and Scholar

Roger Williams
Founder of Rhode Island

John Winthrop
Politician and Statesman

John Peter Zenger
Free Press Advocate

Revolutionary War Leaders

John Adams
Second U.S. President

Ethan Allen
Revolutionary Hero

Benedict Arnold
Traitor to the Cause

King George III
English Monarch

Nathanael Greene
Military Leader

Nathan Hale
Revolutionary Hero

Alexander Hamilton
First U.S. Secretary of the Treasury

John Hancock
President of the Continental Congress

Patrick Henry
American Statesman and Speaker

John Jay
First Chief Justice of the Supreme Court

Thomas Jefferson
Author of the Declaration of Independence

John Paul Jones
Father of the U.S. Navy

Lafayette
French Freedom Fighter

James Madison
Father of the Constitution

Francis Marion
The Swamp Fox

James Monroe
American Statesman

Thomas Paine
Political Writer

Paul Revere
American Patriot

Betsy Ross
American Patriot

George Washington
First U.S. President

Famous Figures of the Civil War Era

Jefferson Davis
Confederate President

Frederick Douglass
Abolitionist and Author

Ulysses S. Grant
Military Leader and President

Stonewall Jackson
Confederate General

Robert E. Lee
Confederate General

Abraham Lincoln
Civil War President

William Sherman
Union General

Harriet Beecher Stowe
Author of Uncle Tom's Cabin

Sojourner Truth
Abolitionist, Suffragist, and Preacher

Harriet Tubman
Leader of the Underground Railroad

Colonial Leaders

George Whitefield

Clergyman and Scholar

Susan Martins Miller

Arthur M. Schlesinger, jr.
Senior Consulting Editor

Chelsea House Publishers

Philadelphia

Produced by Pre-Press Company, Inc., East Bridgewater, MA 02333

CHELSEA HOUSE PUBLISHERS
Editor in Chief Stephen Reginald
Production Manager Pamela Loos
Art Director Sara Davis
Director of Photography Judy L. Hasday
Managing Editor James D. Gallagher
Senior Production Editor J. Christopher Higgins

Staff for *GEORGE WHITEFIELD*
Project Editor Anne Hill
Associate Art Director Takeshi Takahashi
Series Design Keith Trego

The Chelsea House World Wide Web address is http://www.chelseahouse.com

First Printing
1 3 5 7 9 8 6 4 2

Library of Congress Cataloging-in-Publication Data

Miller, Susan Martins.
   George Whitefield / Susan Martins Miller
      p. cm. — (Colonial leaders)
   Includes bibliographical references and index.
   ISBN 0-7910-5967-7 (HC); 0-7910-6124-8 (PB)
     1. Whitefield, George, 1714–1770—Juvenile literature. 2. Church of
   England—Clergy—Biography—Juvenile literature. 3. Great Awakening—
   History—Juvenile literature. [1. Whitefield, George, 1714–1770. 2. Clergy.
   3. Great Awakening. 4. United States—Church history—To 1775.]
   I. Title II. Series.

BX9225.W4 M55 2000
269'.2'092—dc21
[B]   00-038402

Publisher's Note: In Colonial and Revolutionary War America, there were no standard rules for spelling, punctuation, capitalization, or grammar. Some of the quotations that appear in the Colonial Leaders and Revolutionary War Leaders series come from original documents and letters written during this time in history. Original quotations reflect writing inconsistencies of the period.

Contents

Gloucester, England, was where George Whitefield was born and raised. In Gloucester, George developed his early interest in religion. The town was also a constant reminder of the differences between the rich and the poor. Gloucester became a favorite playground of the aristocracy, while the townsfolk struggled to make a living.

A Blue Apron and Dirty Dishes

Two horses clip-clopped down the road, pulling a fine carriage behind them. Inside the carriage were people who lived in a fancy house. At home, a cook prepared their meals and servants brought them food on china plates. Servants also kept the fires going so the house would be warm and maids kept everything in the house clean.

On this cold winter night, a special driver guided the horses. The rich people who sat inside the warm carriage were on their way to see a play in Gloucester, England. They often went to see plays or concerts in Gloucester.

During the early 1700s in England, most people were not so lucky and did not get to see plays and concerts. Average people worked long days at their jobs. It was still dark in the morning when they went to work and it was dark again when they got home at night. They did not get to take vacations. If they got sick and could not work, they did not get paid. Children often started working at a very young age. School was only a dream for them. Their families needed the extra money that they could earn. Before long, these children thought they were too old to bother going to school.

Wealthier people had a comfortable life. They had enough money to buy everything they needed. But most people were not rich and they had a very hard life. More and more people became poor. English farmers in the first part of the century had very small harvests, and there was not enough food to go around. The rich people had money to buy food but the poor people did not.

People who were very, very poor lived in special places called poorhouses. Some children who had no parents lived in orphanages. Many children lived in the streets. They had no homes at all. With no one to take care of them, they had to take care of themselves, sometimes stealing food to eat. As poor as the children were, not everyone felt sorry for them. Some people were cruel to the children. A few rich people tried to help the poor people. But many rich people just wished the poor children would disappear. They did not think the poor children were their problem to solve.

The **aristocracy**—a group of people having wealth and high social status—made all the decisions for the city. The poor people did not get to make any such decisions. They had to do whatever the aristocracy decided. This did not seem fair, but the poor people did not believe they could change anything.

Gloucester, England, became a popular place. The city had many fine buildings made of brick or stone, not just small wooden houses. The buildings had large, comfortable rooms. The Gloucester Spa was a place where natural spring water came up through the ground. Members of the aristocracy liked to come to Gloucester and enjoy the spa. People also came from all around to see plays or go to concerts, especially in the winter.

Many people who could afford to see plays in Gloucester liked to stay at the Bell Tavern and Inn. Thomas and Elizabeth Whitefield owned the inn, which had three stories with many rooms for guests. The dining room was very busy and included a stage that was often used for entertainment. People came from all around to eat and see a show. In the cold winters, a great roaring fire welcomed visitors. The concerts, plays, and nice atmosphere made people want to come to Bell Tavern and Inn. Thomas and Elizabeth Whitefield had a good business. They were not as rich as the aristocracy, but they were not poor.

In the 1700s, the town of Gloucester became a popular resort because wealthy people came to visit and take advantage of the healthful properties of the spa waters.

Thomas and Elizabeth had seven children. The first five children were boys. They then had a daughter. Their last child, a boy named George, was born on December 16, 1714. This was a time when many families were struggling. Thomas and Elizabeth Whitefield made sure their children had food and clothes and a safe place to sleep. The Whitefields had enough money for the things their family needed.

All of the Whitefield children grew up living in the Bell Tavern and Inn. They saw people come from all over to have a meal or something to drink. They saw many of the shows and concerts at the inn. The Whitefield children knew that their parents worked very hard. The children helped with chores around the inn, too. The whole family had to work together to keep the business going.

When George was two years old, tragedy struck the family. His father died. Now his mother had to take care of seven children by herself while running the inn all alone. She worked harder than ever, doing the work of two people. George's older brothers helped even more at the inn. With everyone working together, they kept Bell Tavern and Inn open.

Even though she worked very hard and needed help from them, Mrs. Whitefield wanted her children to go to school whenever they

In order to help his family get by, George would help around the inn— clearing tables, washing dishes, and cleaning the guests' rooms.

could. She made sure that George, her youngest son, received a good education so that someday he would be someone special. Perhaps George would even become the minister of a church. George attended school at a big church in Gloucester. The name of his school was St. Mary de Crypt Grammar School. Sometimes

George Whitefield kept a journal for most of his life. He formed the habit of writing down what he did every day. We know he wore a blue apron and washed dishes at the Bell Inn because he wrote about that and many other details in his journal. George also wrote about the ideas he thought were important. He used his journal to help think about big decisions. His own words tell us a lot about what he did and how he felt. His journals fill many volumes and thousands of pages.

George skipped school because he wanted to play. But he also was a good student and enjoyed learning. His best subject was Latin. George also discovered that he was a good actor. He liked to give special readings or take roles in plays at school. The teachers chose George to make speeches to the city leaders when they visited the school.

When George was eight years old, his mother got married again. Her new husband's name was Mr. Longden. George and his siblings now had a new stepfather, and at first, everyone thought he would help at Bell Tavern and Inn. George's mother was relieved to have the help of a husband again. Mr. Longden wanted to help and to be in charge, but he did not really know how to do the job. Before long, the business was struggling, and the inn was losing money.

George's mother kept working hard, but her new husband made her job harder. The whole family was unhappy. All around them, neighbors were struggling and poor. The Whitefields were in danger of becoming poor themselves. They kept hoping that things would get better. But every year things got worse.

After a few years, George's stepfather decided he did not want to be part of the family anymore. He moved away, and the family did not see him again. Now George's oldest brother, who was grown-up, was in charge of Bell Tavern and Inn. The family worked hard again to save the business.

When George was 15, he dropped out of school to work at the inn. His mother did not want him to leave school but George insisted. He liked going to school, but he knew that his family needed him. He wanted to do his part to help. So every day he would get up and put on his blue apron. He cleared tables in the busy dining room, washed dishes in the kitchen, and cleaned the rooms where the guests stayed.

George worked at the inn for about a year and a half. His oldest brother turned out to be a good businessman, and profits at the Bell Tavern and Inn improved. But it would take a long time to make up for what they had lost.

While he worked at the inn, George always hoped that he would be able to go back to school. Several of his father's relatives had attended Oxford University. George also wanted to go to Oxford. His mother wanted him to go there, too. The problem was that the family could not afford to send him to the university. So George kept working at the Bell Tavern and Inn while he waited for a chance to go to Oxford.

About this time, George became interested in religion. He began to wonder if he could have a career in the **Church of England.** His mother thought this was a wonderful idea. But George could not do that unless he graduated from a university. If only they could find a way for him to go to Oxford.

While attending Oxford, George spent his time involved with studies or serving the needs of wealthier students. As he continued his course work at Oxford, many events occurred which shaped his faith in God and directed the course of his religious beliefs.

2

Sage Tea
—with
No Sugar

George Whitefield's chance to attend Oxford University finally came. George's mother learned from a young man that some special students could go to Oxford as **servitors,** a special kind of student who did not have to pay very much money to attend classes. The family had finally found a way to be able to afford to send George to the university.

At the age of 16, George left his job working at the inn so that he could go back to school and prepare for the university. Two years later, in 1732, George entered Oxford University.

From his years working at the inn, George was used to waiting on people. As a servitor at Oxford, he worked for three or four other students who came from rich families. George washed their clothes and shined their shoes. He ran errands and brought them food. Sometimes he even did their homework for them. George's job was to do whatever the rich students wanted him to do. They gave him some of their old clothes to wear. Every now and then, they paid him a little bit of money. George was never sure if he would have enough money for the things he needed.

Servitors wore special gowns over their clothes. This helped the other students know who they were. Servitors were not allowed to speak to the regular students, and the regular students did not speak to servitors. For a long time, George did not have many friends at Oxford. But none of this mattered to him. He was just glad to finally be at the university. At last he was working toward his dream. He might some day have a career in the Church of England.

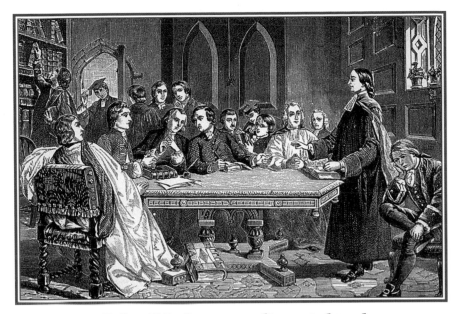

John Wesley, standing right, shown here with the Holy Club, became a close friend of George Whitefield while both attended Oxford. Wesley would later go on to become a prominent leader of the Methodist Church.

George's interest in religion led him to find friends who also were religious. After he had been at Oxford for about a year, he met two brothers named John and Charles Wesley. They were the leaders of the **Holy Club**–a group of young men who shared an interest in religion

John and Charles Wesley went on to become famous religious leaders after they left Oxford. John is most remembered as a leader of the Methodist Church. Some people in England were not happy with the Church of England. These people joined John Wesley's Methodist Church. John preached hundreds of sermons. Charles also became a preacher, but he is more known for the hundreds of religious songs that he wrote. People in churches still sing his songs today. George Whitefield also helped spread the teaching of the Methodist Church to the American colonies.

and met together to help each other study.

George Whitefield took his religion and his studies very seriously. He was busy every minute of the day, studying hard in his classes and working long hours as a servitor. In spite of his busy schedule, he managed to find time to visit people who were sick and prisoners who were lonely and could not live with their families. George did not have very much money, but he gave some to people even poorer than he was.

All of the members of the Holy Club got up very early every morning, trying never to waste a single moment of the day. They met to read the

Bible and pray together. The young men helped each other plan their days, making every minute full. At night, they wrote in their journals. As they wrote, they went over everything that had happened during the day. They made sure they were working hard enough.

More than anything else, George wanted to please God by spending long hours praying. He would sometimes stretch out on the ground and pray, staying there for two or three hours at a time. Even on the coldest days, he would pray outside. No matter how cold or wet he got, he prayed for a long time.

George also believed God wanted him to give up those things that made his life comfortable. He wore shabby clothes and dirty shoes. He stopped eating fruit and sweets and tried not to talk any more than he had to. He wanted to make sure that everything he did would please God.

In the spring of 1735, George decided that he would eat only bread and drink only sage tea.

He did not even allow himself to put sugar in his tea. Serious about this decision, he would not change his mind and had only bread and tea for six weeks. During this time, George grew thin and sick. He became too weak to work as a servitor or to go to his classes. Eventually, he was too weak to even get out of bed. His friends became worried about him. They understood that he wanted to keep his promise to God, but they were afraid he would get so sick that he could not get better. At last, someone called a doctor.

The doctor told George that he must start eating again. He also told him that he was too sick to stay in school and that he should go home to Gloucester until he was healthy again. George was so sick that he had to obey the doctor. He went home to Gloucester.

While he was recovering, George's interest in religion grew, but he began to have some new ideas. He realized that making himself sick was not the way to please God. Instead, all he

Doctors in the 18th century did not have the advantage of the medical training of today's doctors. Still, it was a doctor that helped George restore his health by telling him to follow a normal diet and go back home to Gloucester.

needed to do was receive God's love. George came to believe that God cared for him, that he did not have to earn God's love but just accept it. This belief changed George's life. Now he realized he could serve God and also show his love of God by leading a normal life.

George felt a great sense of relief. He wrote, "God was pleased to remove the heavy load."

As soon as he was well enough, George began **preaching** around the Gloucester area. He preached to anyone who would listen to him. He soon discovered that people liked to listen to him. People began to admire George Whitefield. Soon, holding religious meetings was almost a full-time job for him. He also continued to pray for hours at a time. He got up at 5 A.M. to pray and study the Bible. But now it was for a different reason. He was not afraid that he could not please God. Instead, he wanted to show that he loved God.

Many people started to think that a young man with such enthusiasm for religion should have a career in the church. This was what George had always hoped for. Now that he knew that God loved him, he wanted to work in the church even more.

Bishop Benson in Gloucester was a leader in the Church of England. He noticed George

Whitefield, who was only 20 years old, and saw the talent and great enthusiasm for religion that he had. He saw how popular George was. Bishop Benson began to think that George Whitefield could be a great church leader. He encouraged George to think about becoming a **priest** in the Church of England. He promised to help George with his career after he finished college.

While he was in Gloucester, George remained friends with John and Charles Wesley. They were getting ready to go to the American colonies. They wanted to go there and tell people their beliefs about God. John and Charles hoped that George would go to America with them.

George wanted to go to America and be with his friends, but he decided it was better to wait until after he finished college. In October 1735, John and Charles Wesley left for America. George promised that he would join them as soon as he could.

This building, the Radcliffe Camera in Oxford, was probably under construction when George Whitefield graduated from Oxford in 1736.

After staying in Gloucester for about nine months, George was well enough to return to Oxford. He worked hard to catch up on the studies that he missed. Before long, in June 1736, he was able to graduate.

Bishop Benson remembered the promise he made to George and gave him a job in a church. After he had some experience working in a church, George could become a priest. However, he had not forgotten about his friends John and Charles Wesley. Perhaps working with them in America would also be good experience. George did not feel ready to take on the big responsibility of being the leader of a church. He believed he still had many things to learn.

George began to think more and more about going to America. He wanted to join John and Charles Wesley and be a **missionary** in the colony of Georgia.

George Whitefield's preaching became quite popular in colonial America. His sermons soon began to attract people from many miles away. His clear, booming voice and ability to persuade even the most stubborn listener only added to his celebrity.

3

Orphans and Great Crowds

More than a year passed before George Whitefield left for the American colony of Georgia. He preached in several cities in England, but he still had his mind on going to Georgia. Finally, he traveled on a ship to America in the early part of 1738. His ship passed another ship in the middle of the ocean. John Wesley was on the other ship. He was on his way back to England. John's work in Georgia had not gone well. He thought perhaps he had made a mistake in going to America. Before long, his brother Charles gave up on the work in Georgia, too.

George did not know that his friend John was on his way back to England. He was still full of hope about doing God's work in America. But he did not wait until he got to America to start preaching. Before his ship even left England, George was meeting other people on the ship. He wanted to find out what he could do to help them. After the ship sailed, some travelers became seasick. George visited them and gave them sage tea with sugar. This helped to settle their sick stomachs. George also had some gifts of food and medicine from his friends in London. He gave these away to people on the ship.

Even though he was busy with all these things, George couldn't help but preach. He gathered the officers and soldiers together and held religious meetings for them. George wrote about everything that happened on the ship in his journal.

When the ship had been at sea for about a month, it almost ran into another ship. The captain just happened to be on deck when the danger came. Quickly he steered his ship out of the path of the other ship. Later he told George that he had never been so close to death. He believed that the God that George preached about had kept the ship safe. He asked George to hold public meetings for everyone on the ship to pray together and listen to George preach. Of course, George was very happy to do that. Two other ships were traveling nearby. Sometimes George would stand on the deck and preach loudly enough that all the people on the three ships could hear him.

When fever swept over the ship, people who were already seasick became more sick. George continued to visit everyone who was sick. He caught the fever and became very ill himself. For several days, he was dangerously close to death. Fortunately, he recovered.

George finally reached Savannah, Georgia, in May of 1738. He was still quite sick, but he got up early the first morning he was in the colony. He held his first religious service in

After arriving in Savannah, George began preaching to the colonists the very next day. Although the crowds he preached to seemed small at first, he created quite a stir in the colony and soon attracted thousands of listeners to his sermons.

Savannah. Forty-two people came to hear him. In England, George had preached to larger crowds. Georgia had been a colony for only six years, and not many people lived there. But George wanted to reach the people who were there. Preaching to small groups or large crowds, he just wanted to tell people about God's love.

He discovered that the people in Savannah thought that John Wesley was too strict about religion. That was why they stopped coming to church. But George soon had a dif-

The people in Savannah, Georgia, found John Wesley too strict in his views on religion.

ferent problem. He looked like an ordinary person, but his voice was not ordinary. Long before microphones and electric sound systems were invented, thousands of people could listen to George Whitefield at one time. He had a deep-toned, clear, melodious voice that made people love to listen.

It was not long before he attracted large crowds again. Hundreds, if not thousands, of people came to hear him speak. People came from 40 or 50 miles away, which was a great distance at that time just to hear a speaker. He was invited to come and preach all over Georgia. He accepted as many invitations as he could. Soon George was holding 30 religious meetings every week.

The young colony did not have any big fancy churches for George to preach in. No building was large enough for the crowds that came. So George conducted **open air preaching**, sometimes before crowds as large as 20,000 people. George's marvelous voice carried so far that everyone could hear him clearly. Despite the busy schedule, George showed no signs of getting tired. When he saw a crowd gathered to listen to him, he was filled with fresh energy. He did not want to disappoint anyone who wanted to listen to him. So he always preached to the crowd that gathered.

While he was in Savannah, George Whitefield began working on a project that would be important to him for the rest of his life. He discovered that some of the early settlers in Savannah had died and left behind children who were now orphans. They had no one to take care of them. George remembered what it was like in Gloucester, England, where some children had no place to live. He wanted the orphans in Georgia to have a better life. He believed school was also important. Education had given George a chance to have the career he wanted. He hoped the

Despite his success as a preacher, George never forgot the orphans. Wherever he went, he collected money to help them. During the next 30 years, he gave $16,000 of his own money to the orphanage. In the 1700s, that was a great deal of money. He raised much more than that from other people. He made sure the orphans had a school to go to as well.

Over the years, George had a dream that the orphanage and school might become a university. He made all the plans for his dream to come true. But he died before it happened. A few years after his death, the Revolutionary War began. The school was forced to close because of the war, never to reopen again.

orphans could have the same chance. The children needed a safe place to live and a good school to attend.

As soon as he could, George opened several schools and an orphanage, which he simply called Orphan House. George dreamed of a comfortable building large enough for all the children who needed a home. He imagined how exciting life could be for them if they had someone to take care of them. But George had very little money of his own, and he could not afford to build an orphanage and take care of dozens of children. Right away George knew he would have to have help. He would have to go back to England and raise money. But he was determined to return to Georgia again someday and build a real orphanage.

George had another reason for going back to England. He thought that it was time to go through the ceremony that would make him a priest in the Church of England. His friend, Bishop Benson, was eager for George to become a priest and join the leadership of the church. But he could not do that unless he returned to England. George enjoyed being in Georgia. He wanted to finish the job he had begun in Savannah. But he believed he would spend most of his life as a church leader in England. It was time to go home and prepare for that.

After five months of working in Savannah, George decided to return to England. He held one final religious service. The meeting was so crowded that people lined up outside the doors and listened from under the windows. Everyone there that day was glad to hear that George planned to return as quickly as he could.

By the time George reached English soil again, 11 months had passed. He was excited about the work he had done in America and hoped that he could be just as successful in England. A few weeks after returning to England, he was **ordained** as a priest in the Church of England. Right after that, he began traveling around the country preaching.

Before going to America, George had been popular. He hoped and dreamed that his work would continue to go well now that he was a priest. George also looked forward to being with his friends, Charles and John Wesley. As soon as the Wesley brothers learned that George was back, they hurried to London to be with him.

Not everyone was so glad to see George back in England. Some church leaders did not like his informal style of preaching. They did not like the kinds of things George spoke about. George Whitefield had more influence on people than the leaders of the churches. This made them very unhappy with him.

Before going to America, George had preached in several churches in London. He hoped that he could go back to those churches to preach and to collect gifts of money for the orphanage in Georgia. But after only two days in London, five churches had already turned him down. They would not allow him to preach in their buildings. Some church leaders let

Upon returning home from America, George was not welcomed by everyone within the Church of England. When he found that many churches had closed their doors to him, he returned to his habit of preaching outdoors and continued to bring in listeners from all across the country.

George know that they wished he would leave England for good.

George decided to try preaching in the open air, the way he had in America. If he could not go to churches, he would find the people himself. He would preach where they were.

He headed for an area called Kingswood near Bristol, England. The people there worked in coal mines and did not have a school or a church. Many of them were poor. Coal mining was very hard work. It was February and very cold, but George went around to all the tiny homes and invited people to come and hear him speak on a Saturday. About 200 people came. Four days later, when he preached again, 2,000 people came. Two days after that, 4,000 people came. Eight days after his first sermon in Kingswood, 10,000 came at one time to hear George Whitefield preach. Soon he was holding 30 meetings every week.

From Kingswood, George went on to preach in the open air in London. The same things happened there. Before long, he was speaking to 30,000 people at a time. When he preached, George also collected money for the orphans in Georgia. He still planned to go back to America.

George bought his ticket for the ship that would take him to America again. He had no idea how much this trip would change his life and the lives of hundreds of thousands of people living in the colonies.

Philadelphia was one of the most prominent cities in colonial America. When
George Whitefield returned to the
colonies, he visited Philadelphia. He made
a number of stops in many of America's
larger cities and continued to draw large
audiences wherever he spoke.

4

The Great Awakening

George Whitefield's second trip to the American colonies first took him to Philadelphia, Pennsylvania, one of the most important cities in colonial America. Many of the leading thinkers of the colonies lived and worked there. George Washington and Ben Franklin were there much of the time. George knew that if he visited Philadelphia, he would be able to learn a lot about how people in America lived. He was very interested to learn about their ideas.

George started preaching right away. Six to eight thousand people came to hear him preach each time he spoke. After Philadelphia, George went to New York for a short visit. One Sunday, he preached to 15,000 people in the morning and 20,000 in the afternoon.

Now George was ready to return to Georgia. He could have traveled by ship and arrived in Georgia quickly, but he chose to travel by land. The trip from New York to Georgia took several weeks. Passing through Pennsylvania, New Jersey, Delaware, Maryland, Virginia, North Carolina, and South Carolina, George and his companions did not always know where they would spend the night. Sometimes they stayed in the homes of wealthy families, and other times, they slept outside or in a crowded room with many other people. Everywhere he went, George preached to the crowds that gathered.

George finally reached Savannah, Georgia, on January 10, 1740. The first thing he wanted to do was start building the orphanage. He rented a large house to use temporarily, while workers built a permanent home for the orphans.

George had gotten permission to use 500 acres of land for the orphanage. He planned to pay for building the orphanage with the money he had collected in England. George made plans for one large building and four smaller ones. He also wanted a barn and a dock for small boats. The land was 10 miles from Savannah, so workers had to clear the land and make a road. George hired every worker he could find in the colony of Georgia to work on his project.

The orphans needed a place to live as well as many more things. George wanted to provide them with a school where the girls would learn sewing and weaving, and the boys would learn carpentry and farming. George wanted all the children to grow up and be able to take care of themselves. On March 25, 1740, George laid the first brick of the main building. He called the place Bethesda House, which means House of Mercy. The building project had finally begun, but it would take a long time. While the workers continued with construction, George decided to return to Philadelphia. While he was there, George met Benjamin Franklin, one of the leaders of the colony of Pennsylvania. The two men developed a friendship that would last more than 30 years.

Ben Franklin once went to hear George preach. He later wrote that the preacher had a "loud and clear voice," and that he spoke his words and sentences so perfectly that even people far away could hear him. Ben Franklin was one of the first people to estimate how far away George's voice could be heard. While George was speaking, Ben walked through the streets of Philadelphia until he could no longer hear George. He estimated that 30,000 people could hear George Whitefield's voice at one time.

When Ben Franklin heard George speak, George wanted to collect money for his orphanage. Ben believed that it would cost less money to build an orphanage in Philadelphia and bring the orphans there. So he was not planning to give anything to George Whitefield and Bethesda

House. Ben had in his pocket a "handful of copper money, three or four silver dollars, and five pistoles in gold." As Ben listened to George speak, however, he began to change his mind. At first he thought he would just give some of his copper money, which was not worth as much as the silver or gold, and then he decided he would give his silver money as well. A few minutes later, Ben decided to give the gold money, also. When the collection was taken, Ben emptied his pockets and gave everything he had.

Another man who came to hear George speak had

George's power of persuasion convinced Ben Franklin (above) to donate money to help George's orphanage in the south. The two also became close friends.

George Whitefield's voice could be heard by thousands of people, but he was not a large man and it was not always easy to see him. A crowd of 30,000 people could easily trample him. To solve such problems, George traveled with a portable boxlike structure that had a small ladder and a platform with bars that crisscrossed all around and formed a sort of cage. Here George would be safe from the eager and pressing crowds. Because he was higher up, more people could see him. When he was finished preaching, George could collapse the crate and take it with him to the next stop.

decided to take all his money out of his pockets before he came. That way, he would have nothing to give. But as he heard George Whitefield preach, he decided he wanted to give something after all. He had to borrow money from someone else to put in the collection.

George had more than a loud voice. He had a way of speaking that made people really think about what he said. Over and over, people were persuaded to change their minds and began to agree with the things George said. They believed in God and wanted to help other people by giving money.

Ben Franklin became a good friend to George. He published some of George's **sermons** so that even more people would learn about George's ideas. The whole Franklin family liked George Whitefield. Ben Franklin's mother-in-law gave money to Bethesda House many times.

George and Ben decided to work on some projects together. Ben wanted to start an **academy** in Philadelphia. This would be a charity school for poor children, and it would also be a place where George could preach. When they built the school, they also included an **auditorium** where George could speak whenever he visited Philadelphia. The school opened in 1751. Four years later, a college was added. Many years later, this school became the University of Pennsylvania, a prestigious school which still exists today.

In the fall of 1740, George decided to spend a few weeks in New England. There, he met several other men who were also preaching to large crowds. In Rhode Island, a man named Jonathan

The University of Pennsylvania began its existence as an academy for poor children. The academy was founded by the combined efforts of both George and his friend, Ben Franklin (a statue of whom is seen above), and slowly grew into the university known today.

Edwards had been preaching ideas that were very much like George's. In Boston, George preached to the largest crowds that had ever gathered in that city. In the famous Boston Common, he preached to 15,000 people, and at Old North Church, thousands of people were turned away. There was no place for them to sit in the church.

In another church, someone broke a board into two pieces to make a seat. But others who heard the board break thought it meant the balcony was falling. Suddenly everyone rushed to get out. The crowd turned into a stampede. Some people threw themselves out of the windows. Five people

Jonathan Edwards preached in New England during the time George was in America. Edwards was a key figure in what would come to be known as the Great Awakening.

were killed and many more were injured. George decided it was better to keep preaching in the open air, where there was always enough room for anyone who wanted to hear him speak.

George stayed in New England for only a few weeks, but his preaching began a **revival** that lasted for a year and a half. Other preachers took up where he left off. During such revivals, many people strengthened their belief in God. They held religious services, read from the Bible, listened to preaching, and sang. George did not know it at the time, but he had helped to begin the Great Awakening. During the 1740s in the American colonies, many people who did not care very much about God took an interest in the Bible. They listened to men like George Whitefield, Jonathan Edwards, and Gilbert Tennent. Colonists decided that these men were right about the kind of relationship people should have with God.

Many of the early settlers in the American colonies traveled great distances because they wanted to worship God in their own ways. Religion was important to them. But by the 1700s, many people did not think about religion very much. Some people went to church, but they did

When George visited the Old North Church in Boston, many in the gathered crowd had to be turned away. After running into more serious problems with holding sermons inside buildings and auditoriums, George returned to his custom of preaching outdoors.

not really believe in God. Religion had become a habit. George did not want religion to be a habit. He wanted to help people learn to understand God and God's love. He wanted them to really believe what the Bible said.

During the 1740s, an **epidemic** of **diphtheria** frightened many people. Victims became sick very rapidly, and many died from the disease. Many farmers were also having trouble with their crops. This caused problems for other people, too, because they depended on the farmers for their food. The 1740s were hard times in the American colonies.

George Whitefield came to America during these hard times and talked to people about God. He told them that God cared about their problems. He told them that they should know God as their friend. More and more people, especially poor people, decided that George was right. A revival swept through New England and spread to the other colonies. George Whitefield helped start the biggest revival in American history.

During colonial times, before the Declaration of Independence and the Revolutionary War, the colonies were independent of each other. Each colony made decisions for the people who lived there. Their rules were not always the same ones found in other colonies. But when George came to America the second time, people in different colonies began working together on projects and planning for special events that would help spread the revival. Their work helped all the colonies. George Whitefield came to America to preach about God, but he ended up changing the way the colonies related to each other.

George left America to return to England on January 16, 1741. At his farewell sermon in Boston, thousands gathered to hear him speak. Little did they know how greatly he had changed the path that the colonies would take.

George Whitefield's presence and the effect of the Great Awakening not only had an impact on the course of religion in the colonies, but also resulted in the founding of many universities and colleges where eager young colonists could pursue their religious studies. Princeton University, which began its existence as the College of New Jersey, was primarily founded for the training of ministers.

A Lasting Legacy

ourteen exciting months had carried George Whitefield through the American colonies, from north to south and back again. At last he returned to England. A few months later, he married Elizabeth James, a widow who lived in Wales. Elizabeth moved to London to be with George. They had a son and named him John. They decided that Elizabeth and John would be better off living in Wales while George traveled and preached. So the family began the journey. It was winter, and the coach that they rode in did not have heat. George and Elizabeth bundled up little John to keep him warm.

They stopped for a few days to visit George's family in Gloucester and stayed at the Bell Inn. While there, baby John became sick. His parents called a doctor, but it was too late. Four-month-old John Whitefield died in the house where his father had been born. He was buried in the cemetery next to the church that George had attended as a boy.

George Whitefield did not have any other children. There was no one to carry on his name. But he left such a strong **legacy** that he is remembered for many things.

George Whitefield is famous for traveling around the American colonies preaching. He was also well-known in his own country of England, where he encouraged many people to think about new ideas. He also traveled and preached in Scotland, Ireland, Wales, Gibraltar, Bermuda, and Holland. Not everyone liked him. On one occasion, in Ireland, a mob threatened to kill him. The people who were with George ran away, leaving him to walk half a mile by himself while angry people threw stones at him. This was not the only time that something like this happened. But such events did not stop George from speaking before large crowds.

America never became George Whitefield's home, but he visited often. His work with the orphans in Georgia kept him coming back. And after his second visit, during the Great Awakening, his popularity had grown, and people wanted him to come back

During his lifetime, George Whitefield preached more than 18,000 sermons—which averages to 500 sermons per year, or about 10 per week. Many of his sermons were published, and they can still be read today. George was also the most traveled preacher of his time. Making a total of seven trips to America, he spent 782 days on ships crossing the ocean between England and America. That means that George spent more than two years of his life on board ships making very long and difficult journeys.

again and again. He changed American history in ways he did not even realize.

The Great Awakening, and the years that followed, bound the American people together in

Even though the Great Awakening made its primary emotional appeal to the poor and less educated, it was also of interest to intellectuals. The new churches opened colleges to train their ministers. Many of these schools still exist today. The College of New Jersey opened in 1746 and later became Princeton University; King's College of New York opened in 1746 and later became Columbia University; the College of Rhode Island opened in 1764 and later became Brown University. Queen's College opened in 1766 and later became Rutgers University in New Jersey; and Dartmouth College in New Hampshire, the last of these, was founded in 1769.

a common cause. Before this time, the colonies did not work together very much. After George Whitefield came, people became involved in a religious revival that happened not just in one colony but everywhere. The colonists began to think that God had a special **destiny** for America. People with ideas about government also began to work together, trying to discover what kind of future America could have.

George's preaching also helped spread ideas about **democracy.** Although he did not talk specifically about democracy in his sermons, he did talk about the importance of every individual, especially to God. Every person thus had to make a decision about their belief in God. The poorer people in the colonies began to realize that their ideas were just as important as the ideas of rich people. Everyone mattered. In some colonies, this way of thinking helped form the ideas that eventually led up to the Revolutionary War.

In many ways, George Whitefield and the Great Awakening changed the way people thought about churches and paved the way for religious freedom in America. In some colonies, the government and the church were connected. This followed the pattern of the government of England being connected to the Church of England. In New England, for instance, Congregational churches were preferred by government leaders. In other colonies, Anglican churches, which were like the Church of England, were the favorites.

During the Great Awakening, the connection between churches and government weakened.

Dartmouth College was founded in 1769 by the Reverend Eleazar Wheelock, a Congregational minister from Connecticut. Wheelock had earlier established a school in Connecticut principally for the education of Native Americans. Seeking to expand his school, he moved to Hanover in the Royal Province of New Hampshire. Samson Occom, a Mohegan Indian and one of Wheelock's first students, helped to raise the funds needed to open the school. In 1769, King George III granted a charter for the school. The original charter created a college "for the education and instruction of Youth of the Indian Tribes in this land . . . and also of English Youth and others."

The churches were divided over what they thought about George Whitefield and other preachers. Nicknames were given to the various groups. The **Old Lights** were the people who sided with established churches. They were not happy about revivals and thought they were too emotional and not serious enough. The **New Lights** were the people who followed the revival preachers. Some of them started their own churches.

George Whitefield's seventh and last trip to America began in 1769. As he grew older, his health got worse, and he had to strug-

Dartmouth College was one of the many colleges and universities founded following the Great Awakening. During this time, the majority of learning still centered around the Bible, and colleges such as Dartmouth were created to help serve this growing interest and provide new ministers for the churches.

gle to keep up his energy. He gained weight, and people thought that he looked tired. Still, George did not slow down his preaching schedule. As always, when he arrived in America, he checked on Bethesda House, the orphanage in Georgia. Everything was being very well taken care of. George had raised enough money to pay off the debts of the orphanage and begin construction on new buildings. He also dreamed of having a college at Bethesda House.

He then set out on a preaching tour that took him to Philadelphia, New York, and New England. Everywhere he went, he was received by huge crowds waiting to hear him preach. However, with every day that passed he grew more tired. George had hoped to travel to Canada and preach there for the first time. But his health was getting worse, and he decided to return to Georgia.

On September 29, 1770, he stopped in the town of Exeter on his way to Boston. He was planning simply to rest and continue his journey. But a crowd gathered, and he did not want to disappoint them. As he walked to his platform in the middle of a field, an old man told him that he looked like he should be in bed. George agreed, but he did not go to bed. He climbed up onto the preaching platform and preached for two hours. Later, some people said that it was the best sermon he ever preached. He said:

> Lord Jesus, I am weary in thy work, but not of thy work. If I have not yet finished my course, let me go and speak for thee once more in the fields, seal thy truth, come home and die.

George then went home with a friend who lived in Newburyport, Massachusetts. While the family was eating supper, George said he was too tired to eat and would like to go to bed. Anyone who looked at him could see that he was very sick.

When he was halfway up the stairs to his bedroom, George discovered that a crowd had gathered outside the home. Someone opened the door. Once again, George did not want to disappoint the people who had come to hear him preach. Holding a candle in his hand on the stairs, he preached until the candle burned out.

Finally, George went to bed. During the night he struggled to breathe, he told his friend: "My asthma is returning; I must have two or three days' rest . . . I am dying."

By early morning on September 30, 1770, George Whitefield had died. He was a few weeks short of being 56. His funeral was held on October 2 at the Old South First Presbyterian Church. Thousands of people were not even able to get near the door.

When news of his death reached England, his longtime friend John Wesley preached at the official memorial service:

> Oh what has the church suffered in the setting of that bright star which shone so gloriously in our hemisphere. We have none left to succeed him; none of his gifts; none anything like hime in usefulness.

George Whitefield kept his heart and mind focused on one thing for all of his life. He wanted only to preach about God and to show other people how they could find spiritual fulfillment. Along the way, George changed the way people felt about religion and what they thought about their new country. Although he never lived permanently in America, George was one of the most influential leaders in the new colonies.

GLOSSARY

academy a school

aristocracy a group of people who have high social status because of the wealthy families they are born into

auditorium a room used for speeches and other public gatherings

Church of England the Christian church in England that is recognized by the government as the national church

democracy a system of government where every person's vote counts in an election

destiny the fortune or fate of a person or thing

diphtheria a disease caused by bacteria that may affect the heart and nervous system

epidemic a rapid spreading of disease

Holy Club a religious group of men led by John Wesley at Oxford University

legacy what a person is remembered for after death

missionary a person who explains a religion and invites other people to join it

New Lights people in the 1740s who followed the new teachings of revival preachers

Old Lights people in the 1740s who agreed with established churches

open air preaching speaking on a religious subject out in the open, not in a building

ordained to be officially recognized as a minister in a Christian church

GLOSSARY

preach to speak publicly on a religious subject

priest a minister in certain kinds of churches

revival an increase of interest in religion by a number of people

sermon a public talk on a religious subject

servitor a servant or attendant

CHRONOLOGY

1714 George Whitefield is born on December 16.

1717 George's father dies.

1723 George's mother marries Mr. Longden.

1730 George leaves school to work at the inn.

1732 Enters Oxford.

1733 Meets John and Charles Wesley and joins the Holy Club.

1735 Becomes ill and leaves Oxford.

1736 Graduates from Oxford.

1738 Goes to America for the first time; stays four months.

1739 Ordained as priest in Church of England; preaches in the open air in England.

1740 Goes to America for second time; builds Bethesda House.

1741 Marries a widow, Elizabeth James, on November 14.

1743 Only son, John, dies at four months.

1744 Begins third visit to America.

1751 Visits America for the fourth time; builds academy in Philadelphia.

1754 Begins fifth visit to America.

1763 Takes sixth visit to America.

1769 Travels to America for the seventh time.

1770 George Whitefield dies on September 30 in Newburyport, Massachusetts.

COLONIAL TIME LINE

1607 Jamestown, Virginia, is settled by the English.

1620 Pilgrims on the *Mayflower* land at Plymouth, Massachusetts.

1623 The Dutch settle New Netherlands, the colony that later becomes New York.

1630 Massachusetts Bay Colony is started.

1634 Maryland is settled as a Roman Catholic colony. Later Maryland becomes a safe place for people with different religious beliefs.

1636 Roger Williams is thrown out of the Massachusetts Bay Colony. He settles Rhode Island, the first colony to give people freedom of religion.

1682 William Penn forms the colony of Pennsylvania.

1688 Pennsylvania Quakers make the first formal protest against slavery.

1692 Trials for witchcraft are held in Salem, Massachusetts.

1712 Slaves revolt in New York. Twenty-one blacks are killed as punishment.

1720 Major smallpox outbreak occurs in Boston. Cotton Mather and some doctors try a new treatment. Many people think the new treatment shouldn't be used.

1754 French and Indian War begins. It ends nine years later.

1761 Benjamin Banneker builds a wooden clock that keeps precise time.

1765 Britain passes the Stamp Act. Violent protests break out in the colonies. The Stamp Act is ended the next year.

1775 The battles of Lexington and Concord begin the American Revolution.

1776 Declaration of Independence is signed.

FURTHER READING

Adler, David A. *Benjamin Franklin: Printer, Inventor, Statesman.* New York: Holiday House, 1992.

Davidson, Margaret. *The Story of Benjamin Franklin, Amazing American.* Milwaukee, WI: Gareth Stevens Publishing, 1997.

Fisher, Margaret, and Mary Jane Fowler. *Colonial America.* Grand Rapids, MI: The Fideler Company, 1962.

Fraden, Dennis. *Pennsylvania in Words and Pictures.* Chicago: Children's Press, 1980.

Kalman, Bobbie. *Colonial Times From A to Z.* New York: Crabtree Publishing, 1998.

Knight, James E. *Journey to Monticello: Traveling in Colonial Times.* Mahwah, NJ: Troll Associates, 1982.

Thomas, Kathleen. *Georgia.* Austin, TX: Raintree Steck-Vaughn Publishers, 1996.

INDEX

INDEX

PICTURE CREDITS

page

3: Bettmann/Corbis

6: Dean Conger/Corbis

11: Hulton-Deutsch Collection/ Corbis

13: Used by permission of Keith Pendry, The Bell Inn, Gloucester, England: www.bellinncotswold.com

18: M. Saunders

21: Archive Photos

25: Tate Gallery, London/ Art Resource, NY

28: M. Saunders

30: Francis G. Mayer/Corbis

34: Lee Snider/Corbis

35: Archive Photos

41: Lambert/Archive Photos

44: Archive Photos

49: Archive Photos

52: University of Pennsylvania

53: Archive Photos

55: Richard T. Nowitz/Corbis

58: Lee Snider/Corbis

65: S. Kerekes

ABOUT THE AUTHOR

An avid reader since she first decoded the alphabet, **SUSAN MARTINS MILLER** continues to spin stories, both real and fictional, for readers of all ages. She is the author of more than two dozen books that include fiction and biography for both children and adults, and a nonfiction book about hyperlexia, an unusual developmental disorder. She lives in Colorado Springs, Colorado, with her husband and two children and enjoys the view of Pikes Peak outside her front door.

Senior Consulting Editor **ARTHUR M. SCHLESINGER, JR.** is the leading American historian of our time. He won the Pulitzer Prize for his book *The Age of Jackson* (1945) and again for *A Thousand Days* (1965). This chronicle of the Kennedy Administration also won a National Book Award. He has written many other books including a multi-volume series, *The Age of Roosevelt*. Professor Schlesinger is the Albert Schweitzer Professor of the Humanities at the City University of New York, and has been involved in several other Chelsea House projects, including the REVOLUTIONARY WAR LEADERS biographies on the most prominent figures of early American history.